Acknowledgements

◊ Noreen Wetton and other friends and colleagues at the Health Education Unit of the Research & Graduate School of Education, University of Southampton from whom I have learned so much.

◊ Harriet Smith-Petersen and children from various nursery schools in Hampshire and Surrey for the artwork and cover pictures.

Contents

Acknowledgements   3

Introduction   7

What you get in this book   8

Framework for Circle Time   14

The five PSHE themes   16

Theme 1
Friends and friendships   20

Theme 2
Growing up   36

Theme 3
Feelings and persuasion   52

Theme 4
Keeping safe   68

Theme 5
Citizenship   84

Resources   100

Introduction

Circle Time is widely used as an approach which can help children to gain in confidence and self-esteem. However, most books about Circle Time are for older primary pupils and do not take sufficient account of social and language skills of younger pupils.

This book is different as it focuses on **the early years**.

What size of circle?

This book concentrates on simple activities that can be done by the youngest children in small groups. Most Circle Time books suggest a large circle, but this is not appropriate for very young children who find it easy to tell but hard to listen. It is important that small, easily managed groups give plenty of opportunity for all children to take an active part and have their say. As the pupils mature, and once the format of Circle Time has been established, their improved skills and experience will enable them to respond in larger groups and circles. Until this time children will respond much better in very small groups.

Why PSHE in Circle Time?

Circle Time can become a platform of reassurance for children who need to know there is a time when they can have their say and be listened to. It is important to make sure that the content of Circle Time is interesting and fun but also educational.

Circle Time is a particularly useful tool for physical, social and health education (PSHE) as well as citizenship. Circle Time activities reinforce the importance of turn-taking and sharing the adult's time while at the same time allowing each child to partake in an activity. The activities in this book provide the foundation of PSHE on which later curriculum rests.

In Circle Time young children have the opportunity to:

- listen to others
- be listened to
- talk to the whole group
- improve their social skills
- co-operate with children and adults
- increase their self-confidence
- improve their self-esteem
- get to know their classmates
- improve their friendship-making skills
- identify and voice their own needs
- become aware of the needs of others
- realise that their problems are often common to the group and can be solved.

What you get in this book.

This book has been developed to help you to plan and carry out Circle Time for the youngest children in school. It provides separate activities for:

Nursery/Reception children and Key Stage 1 children.

On the activity pages nursery / reception is on the left page and key stage one is on the right page. You have the flexibility to use activities from either page to suit your group. The suggestion of activities provides a framework to assist emotional development, they are not a strait jacket.

Younger children – 3-5 years

For the youngest children it is essential to start with a small group of no more than ten children. Initially gather them together in a small intimate group sitting round your feet. A circle – even a small circle - is difficult to maintain for very young children and has that large threatening open space between you and them.

A group gives security to the youngest children; as they mature and become more secure in knowing the routine of Circle Time, the group can be enlarged and finally a circular arrangement will be successful.

In nurseries/playgroups where the organisation is of three groups of ten children it is best to have Circle Time in three groups, each controlled by the adult in charge of that group. These three groups could be sited in areas of the nursery where it is quiet enough not to be overheard or influenced by the other groups and take place at the same time. If not, it might be more satisfying to have each group's Circle Time in the quiet area at different times of the day. Even with many 'rising fives' Circle Time will still work better with small numbers – perhaps half the class at a time

Start by having short sessions of ten or fifteen minutes until the children are used to the situation. Follow a regular pattern, so that these young children know what to expect. Always start with:

- a welcome
- then teacher's time
- followed by children's time
- the main theme
- and an ending activity.

Making the 'circle'

Young children may find that work in an open circle is not comfortable and even worrying, being used to making a close group around the teacher for their together times. Circle Time activities fit well into this close-knit formation and teachers may find that this arrangement is easier to handle than a huge open circle.

Where teachers of Nursery/Reception children want to try an open circle it should be small - small enough to allow everyone to take turn without getting bored, certainly no more than ten. Some books on Circle Time suggest using carpet squares – one for each child and these will help the children to stay in one place. Some books suggest using chairs for sitting. Find the arrangement that suits your group but a firm location, either a chair or carpet square, helps locate and maintain a circle.

Older infants 5-8

The older children still need close contact with their teacher, but most will now respond well in larger groups. At six years old the whole class, sitting in a group around you will work quite well. Gradually introduce the Circle Time routine with half the class. Activities such as Pass the Face,

Change Places, Pass the sentence work best in the Circle. When the children can sit in the Circle with the teacher the other activities can be introduced.

Use the same format as for the youngest children, starting with a welcome and ending with a fun session. The theme itself will add variety as it sometimes includes asking the children to do a piece of drawing or writing individually, in pairs or groups which can be shared, explored and extended.

If children are to sit still for the whole of the Circle Time consider carefully the length of time for each session. Young children quickly get bored if they are expected to sit still for long – better to have two short Circle Times of fifteen minutes each than one of half an hour which doesn't work. Longer sessions will work if you have a moving game or activity, e.g. activities which allow children to move about, change places or go off to work in pairs or small groups. This will engage all the pupils' interest, give opportunity for them to move and allow Circle Time to run longer than for more static sessions.

With young KS1 pupils aged 5/6 whole class work is preferable, but could be difficult to maintain in an open circle unless they are particularly mature and can relate to you in this open space. You will still find that a fairly tight group instead of a circle is more easily organised and managed.

Making the circle

For younger KS1 children, if you want to have a circle with the whole class instead of a close group, you might find it useful to try two circles, one inside the other. It is certainly easier to manage the activities (and not miss anyone out) in a circular formation and this allows children to be closer to the teacher than if they were in one huge circle. Initially organise this by making one circle with children from half the class – use half of their working groups. When this group is settled and sitting, ask the other half of the class to make another circle **outside** the first and sit with them there.

You may wish to use small carpet squares for the children to sit on which will keep the shape of the circle and avoid it disintegrating. Some teachers/adults are happy to sit on the floor, choosing their space when the circle has been made. Adults who prefer to sit on a chair should make sure it is a low one, taking steps to make sure that the same children do not always manage to sit by them!

To form one large open circle with older children may mean organising furniture. This is quite possible with older children and does not take too much time as long as you give explicit instructions so that they know exactly what you want them to do. Try Circle Time outside on the grass in the summer.

Rules

It is important to set rules for Circle Time. These can be as simple as:
1. Only one person talks at a time.
2. Listen to and look at the person who is talking.
3. Don't touch the people sitting next to you.
4. We don't say things that upset people.
5. You can pass if you need time to think.

(Passing is an important element of Circle Time. If a child chooses to pass at the end of the round ask if the child wants to say anything. You might say "I'm coming back to the children who wanted more time to think, sometimes we need to think carefully before we answer". If the child still chooses to pass be non-judgemental - passing is OK!)

Older pupils can be asked to suggest Circle Time rules and the class can vote on the ones to select. These can be written up and the children can read through them occasionally – or when it is necessary to remind them.

Signals

Introduce a quietening signal at the start of each session as the children will come bubbling to the circle. Making a loud noise, shouting above the general noise of the children or singling out one noisy child is not a good idea. Most teachers will have their recognised signal for quiet and will use that. Some teachers sing and clap to a musical "Are you ready?" and children can sing and clap the response "Yes we are". Other signals can be a raised hand, folded arms, sitting quietly, looking at everyone. Use the same signal after children have been talking in pairs or small groups.

With older pupils select some tangible object to be passed round the circle, giving permission to speak in the round. Tell the children that this is what people used to do in the olden days when the Elders of the village had their meetings. Choose a special object only used for this purpose – e.g. a baton, large shell, pseudo microphone - or use various appropriate objects according to the content of the Circle Time.

Explain that in reply to questions generated by the group, a raised hand gains the floor and that shouting out the answer is not acceptable. It is not always easy to ignore the excited child who shouts out or thrusts a hand into view but, if adults are consistent in their response, children will soon learn what is acceptable.

It is useful to start each session by reminding the children of the rules; you could have written up nearby. Before each session you could read them or ask for a reading volunteer to read them.

Listening Skills

Right from the start explain that when someone is talking it is everyone's job to really listen. Children will need to learn the skill of really listening – this involves looking at the person talking – looking at their eyes or their mouth.

Make up some games to improve this skill – such as:

- speak without sound and ask the children to tell you what they think your lips have said
- use facial expressions to show how you are feeling and ask the children to tell you
- play 'Chinese Whispers' with a small group in the middle of the circle or group.

<u>Chinese Whispers</u> - With no more than five children in a line, whisper a short phrase which the child will repeat to the next person, s/he repeats to the next and so on until the last child speaks it out loud. Then the teacher says out loud what the first whisper has been.

Insist that the children look at the child/adult talking, making sure the children don't comment or interrupt until that person has finished.

Children will need help to concentrate and think about what the person means when they are talking.

Only allow the next speaker to talk when they have used your recognised signal – a raised hand, a raised finger, or whatever signal is used.

Explain to children that we can tell when they are really listening, by the way they look. The adult can demonstrate this by their own and other children's body language – nodding, smiling, frowning, showing sympathy.

These skills do not come easily to young children, but Circle Time is an ideal opportunity for children to learn the skill of effective listening.

Co-operation

Circle Time can only operate well if all the children co-operate and engage in appropriate behaviour. There will be children who find it difficult to concentrate or who distract other children. There are various ways to deal with this, such as:

- stop the session and remind the group of the rules
- explain that Circle Time is only possible with their concentration and co-operation
- if children are distracting others, ask them to change places with someone else, explaining why this is necessary
- be tough, but only ever exclude children from the group if there is some other supervised activity they can do – making sure this is not a 'treat'. Remind them you are asking them to leave because they are not following the rules. If they re-join the group welcome them back and note your pleasure that they are coming back and will now follow the rules of the "circle".
- when it is necessary to give a warning, only give it once and then carry out your warning.

It takes quite a lot of skill to run Circle Time effectively with young children if real learning is to take place. Time taken in the early stages to establish the format and organisation of Circle Time is not wasted and will pay dividends in future sessions. Those who experience difficulties may need to shorten the session or look carefully at the content. Make it lively and fun and children will respond well and look forward to Circle Time.

Schools develop Circle Time in their own way. The following framework provides guidelines which are meant to be used flexibly. Schools which have a well developed ethos of Circle Time could add to this framework.

The following Lucky Duck publications might be useful in assisting staff to gain confidence in using Circle Time and ensuring that progression is developmental.

Circle Time   Developing Circle Time
6 Years of Circle Time   Magic Circles
Coming Round to Circle Time (video)   Circle Time Resources
Circle Time for the Very Young.

Framework for Circle Time

It is important to create a regular format for the sessions – it helps to organise time and gives children a routine to expect.

1. Welcome

Start by saying hello to each child by name – "Good morning James" with each child replying 'Good morning Mrs. Whatever'.

2. Teachers' time

If there is anything special to say such as recognising a child's birthday or remarking on something, this is the time to do it. Keep this short.

3. Children's time

Ask the children if there is anything they want to tell. By giving the tangible object to each child who is speaking preserves the right for that child to speak. It is often necessary to limit the number of children who can hold the floor – say 5 each session. Other children can come later and tell on their own or wait until the next Circle Time. It is important to keep this section lively.

4. Themes

There are 5 main PSHE themes in this book:
1. Friends and Friendship
2. Growing Up
3. Feelings and Persuasion
4. Keeping Safe
5. Citizenship.

These are subdivided into 40 topics –one a week for a school year. Each topic has two sections on facing pages, one for the youngest children 3-5 and one for older children 5-8.

Older children are sometimes asked to draw a picture and if possible to write some words before they come to the group. This is then shared with the group. Children put their picture on a pile after showing it. Children who (for any reason) do not want to show their picture can 'pass' and just add theirs to the pile.

Each topic has suggestions for further work which often includes ideas for a display of children's work.

The activities are interchangeable and can be used to suit the abilities and skills of the children you work with – you can mix and match them. Teachers of children with special needs or those in special schools can find the appropriate level for their pupils.

5.   Songs, games, or various fun endings

Most teachers have a repertoire of songs, poems, games and ring games. This is a relaxing way to end each session. With younger children use nursery rhymes or counting games – e.g. "Five brown buns" (traditional) , "One elephant" (Okki-Tokki Unga). There is a list of songbooks for young children at the end of this book.

Organising Groups

Many of the activities are arranged as small group work. One of the strengths of Circle Time Activities is that children can be arranged in groups that don't follow their normal friendship groups. Rather than say "get into groups of five" where children will seek out their friends, arrange the groups. The following games might be helpful.

Mixing up Games

Go round the circle and give each child a designation:

Train, boat, plane (transport)

Apple, orange, banana, cherry, plum (fruit)

Lion, cat, dog, rabbit (animal.)

At any time you can say: "trains, stand up and change places", or "boats, stand up and change places. If you say "transport", everyone will change places. These act as energisers, change the social groupings, but also act as a quick way of organising groups for small group work. "I want all trains to go to that corner, boats will work here and planes sit next to the blackboard."

The five PSHE Themes

These activities are intended to be slotted into Circle Time after 'Children's time' and before your fun ending.

Theme 1 Friends and friendships

1. Who I am
2. What is a friend?
3. Being a good friend
4. New friends, old friends
5. Quarrels
6. Making Up
7. Making others happy
8. When friends move – separation.

Theme 2 Growing up

1. When I was very young
2. Now I am .... I can…
3. Looking back
4. It takes time to grow
5. I know I'm getting bigger because…
6. Who helps us to grow and learn
7. New responsibilities
8. Looking forward.

Theme 3 Feelings and persuasion

1. Feeling good
2. Feelings we share
3. How can we tell how people are feeling?
4. Feelings change
5. Feeling afraid –what can we do?
6. Good persuasion
7. Bad persuasion
8. Saying 'no' to bad persuasion.

Theme 4 Keeping safe

1. Who am I?
2. Who keeps me safe?
3. I can keep myself safe.
4. At home
5. Outside
6. Keeping my body healthy and safe
7. People I need to keep safe from
8. Our messages about keeping safe.

Theme 5 Citizenship

1. Why do we need rules?
2. Rules outside school.
3. Who makes the rules?
4. Other people's property and feelings
5. Being truthful
6. Losing and Finding
7. Litter
8. Protect our environment.

Explanation of terms

Pass the sentence. Sometimes the adult starts by making a statement and asking a question to a nearby child. The child responds and asks the same question to another child, thus passing on the sentence. (See Friends and Friendships '*Who am I*' for first use).

Hands up session – an opportunity for children to offer ideas by raising their hands – i.e. not going round the circle/group.

Stand and show – children sitting with pictures or work individually stand up to show their work and sit down before another child stands.

Pass the face – see explanation in Friends and Friendships '*Being a good friend*'

Change places – when children are asked to offer words/phrases (in Pass the sentence or other activities) a child may repeat a word/phrase that has already been said by another child. To give movement to the session ask the second child to change places with the child who first gave the word. When the same words are offered several times ask the child to change places with the child who most recently gave the word. (See Friends and Friendship '*Quarrels*' for first use.)

Jot down – have a notebook or piece of paper with you and jot down some of the appropriate words/phrases the children offer you. You can discuss these with the children after the activity, rather than break the flow at the time. You may be able to use these words later in the activity.

Themes and Activities

1. Friends and Friendship
2. Growing Up
3. Feelings and Persuasion
4. Keeping Safe
5. Citizenship.

1. Who I am

There are many variations of this game, you can suit it to the children in your class. The main object is to be able to tell something positive about yourself and ask a friend. Here are three different questions you can use. They all follow the same format as the first one.

<u>Question and answer</u>
<u>Who are you?</u>
> Tell the nearest child who you are and ask who she is.
> "I am Mrs. Jones, who are you?"
> The child replies
> "I am John."
> John turns from you and says to the nearest child
> "I am John, who are you?"

Pass this on round the group/circle.

I like playing ball with Kate.

Jodie

> What are you good at?
> "I am Mrs. Jones and I am good at playing tennis. What are you good at doing?"
> "I am James and I am good at running. What are you good at doing?"

> What do you like doing?
> "I like reading books, what do you like doing?"
> "I like playing in the playhouse, what do you like doing?"

<u>Further work</u>
> Talk about what other people like to do. Ask children to draw themselves doing something they like to do. You could make a display of the children's drawings with the heading "This is what we like to do".

1. Who I am

Ask the children to work in pairs to find out one thing about their friend. Allow only a couple of minutes for this and reform the group or circle. (In this way children can explore what others in the class like or dislike, realising that personal preference is OK – we don't all have to like the same things.)

<u>Pass the sentence</u>
"My friend … likes…"

Start the game by saying what a friend of yours likes.
"My friend Mary likes to sew."
Ask a child   *"What does your friend like?"*
The child replies and then turns to the next person with the same question.

My friend Azif likes playing football.

Rafe

Progressions on this theme could be:
"I like to… but my friend Jim likes to…"
"I don't like to…"
"I don't like to … but my friend Syd does"
"James and I would like to…

<u>Further work</u>
This work can lead to display about likes and dislikes. Children can draw on one half of the paper something they like and on the other half something they don't like. Ask the children to think of a title – perhaps
"We don't all like the same things."

2. What is a friend?

A friend

plays with me
shares things
is kind
likes me
sits by me
helps me.

Ask the children to close their eyes and think of their friends and how they know that these people are friends. Allow half a minute for this.

<u>Pass the sentence.</u>
>   Ask each child in turn to tell you one thing about a friend.
>   *"A friend is…"*

As the children tell you, listen for any key words that tell you what a friend is and jot these down on a paper. Allow children to 'pass' and return to these children when everyone else has had a say. (This gives timid children more time to think.) Allow repeats and second chances to 'pass' if necessary.

>   Read out the list of key words you have made and write these large on a flip chart.
>   Talk about these with the children and ask if they can add any more in a
<u>Hands up</u> session. (i.e. ask children to raise their hand if they can tell you more.)

>   Now read again all their suggestions and ask the children
>   to think of when a friend of theirs did one of these things.

<u>Stand up</u> if you have a friend who …..

This is me sharing a book with my good friend.

Shola

<u>Further work</u>
>   Ask the children to help read the key word list once each day.
>   Children could add to the list by drawing some of the key word actions for you to display around the list (as clues).
>   Ask children to draw a picture of themselves doing something that shows they are a good friend.

2. What is a friend?

Before you start Circle Time ask the children to draw a picture of a good friend and to write round their picture some of the things that their friend does that shows they are a friend.

Come together for Circle Time and ask each child to:
<u>Stand and show</u> their picture to the group and say one of the things that their friend does.
(Each child stands in turn and shows their picture to the group. Allow children to pass.)

<u>Pass the sentence.</u>
The children can finish this sentence in any appropriate way.
"My friend…
As the children are talking make a list of what they say.
At the end of the session read your list to the class and ask if they can group things on your list together in any way or put it into some kind of order.

<u>Further work</u>
You can make a chart of the list of words and use some of the children's pictures to decorate it.
Use the words as aids to spelling or reading practice.
At the next Circle Time session remind the children of the work they did.

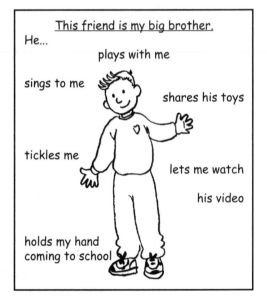

This friend is my big brother.
He…
plays with me
sings to me
shares his toys
tickles me
lets me watch
his video
holds my hand
coming to school

3. Being a good friend

Ask the children to think about what being a good friend is all about.
Ask the children to
stand up if they think they are a good friend.

<u>Pass the sentence</u>
"I am a good friend when I…

Jot down some of key words and make a short list for everyone to see/read.

Look at what they have said and ask them
if they can sort these into groups -
e.g. easy to do, hard to do;

Ask the children to
<u>Stand up if</u>
    they think its easy to be a good friend
<u>Stand up if</u>
    they think its hard to be a good friend.

Being a good friend.

<u>easy</u>
play with them
share with them
talk to them
work with them.

<u>hard</u>
let them be first
let them choose
listen to them
share other friends.

Ask the children to help you to count how many think its easy.
Tell the children it is hard to do what a friend wants to do if you want to do something else.
It gets easier if you can take turns.

<u>Further work</u>
    Ask children to draw themselves being a good friend and add your writing to say what they are doing. (Children could take their pictures home to show their families.)

3. Being a good friend

Ask children to think of a time when they did something to please a friend – perhaps something they didn't want to do, but they did it because they knew their friend wanted them to. Ask all the children to finish this sentence:

<u>Pass the sentence</u>
     "I pleased my friend when I…"

19 of us think its easy to please a friend

10 of us think it can sometimes be hard to please a friend.

     Ask the children to
<u>Stand up if</u>
     it was hard to do that. (Count how many)
<u>Stand up if</u>
     it was easy to do that (Count how many)

Ask the children to think of how their face looked when they were pleasing their friend.
<u>Pass the face</u> round the group/circle, (e.g. the first child makes an appropriate face, shows the
     next person, who turns to show their appropriate face to the next person to them).

<u>Further work</u>
     Ask the children to draw on one half of a piece of paper a picture of their face when
     they were pleasing their friend.
     On the other half they draw a picture of their friend's face.
     You could display these as pairs, or cut and mount them separately.

4. New friends, old friends

Ask the children to think about other friends — not necessarily children friends but new people who have just come into their lives.

<u>Stand up if</u>
> you can think of a new friend.
> Ask them to tell something about this new friend.

<u>Pass the sentence</u>
> "My new friend is … and …"

My new friend is Mr Jones.
He has moved next door.

<u>Stand up if</u>
> you can think of an old friend.
> Ask them to tell something about this old friend.

<u>Pass the sentence</u>
> "My old friend is … and …"

> Now ask them to think about friends who are older than they are— perhaps friends of their family, grandparents or new neighbours.

Auntie May is an old friend.
She saw me when I was a baby.

<u>Pass the sentence</u>
> "A grown-up friend of mine is… and…"

<u>Further work</u>
> Children can draw their old and new friends and add labels or captions to their pictures with your help. This could make a two part display – 'new friends, old friends'.

4. New friends, old friends

Ask children to think about new friends, young or old people they have just met and who they know are going to be friends.

Ask each child to tell one thing about one of these new friends.

<u>Pass the sentence</u>
"My new friend is …. I know we are going to be friends because…"

Now ask the children to think of some friends they have known for a long time – perhaps a friend of their parents. Ask some of the children to tell the group about this friend.

This is my new friend Zoe.

I know we are going to be good friends because we like to play the same games and she lives near me.

Now ask them to think of friends they had for a short time – 'little while friends' perhaps they moved to a new house, or met them on holiday and may never see them again, but they will always remember them.

<u>Pass the sentence</u>
"I remember … because…"

<u>Further work</u>
Look for books in the class/school library about friends such as *"Orlando's little while friends"* by A Wood, published by Child's Play or *Wilfred Gordon McDonald Partridge*, by M. Fox & J Vivas published by Picture Puffins.
Ask the children to draw and write about:
one character in the story
some friend they met once
an imaginary friend they would have liked to have.

5. Quarrels

Talk about why people sometimes quarrel.

Tell a short story about two children who quarrelled.

Jan and Del usually were good friends and usually played well together but one day they both wanted to use the same crayon at the same time and they grabbed for it. They couldn't agree who should have it first and Jan pushed Del who started to cry. The teacher was not pleased with either of them.

Ask the children to think about how Del and Jan felt.

Ask each child to tell you how one of these children felt.

Pass the sentence

"I think Del felt…

or "I think Jan felt…

For variation, ask children who repeat a word that has already been said to **change places** with the first person who said the word. (There will be many words repeated.)

Jot down on paper any useful or appropriate words the children offer.

When all the children have had a turn (or passed!), read out the words they told you.

Write them large on a flip chart or chalk board under the headings **Del** and **Jan.**

Read the words with the children – are any of the words the same in both lists?

Read the words again and ask the children to show by their face how Del felt.

Pass the face around the circle.

Further work

You could explore these feelings and body language in drama sessions.

5. Quarrels

Ask children to close their eyes and think about a time when someone they knew quarrelled. Ask them to think about how they themselves felt when someone quarrelled.

<u>Pass the sentence</u>
"When I saw someone quarrel I felt… (Make sure they don't use people's names)
Children who repeat a word **change places** with the first person who said it

Ask the children to think of their own quarrels and choose one of the following.
<u>Pass the sentence</u>
"When someone quarrelled with me I felt…
"When I quarrelled with someone I felt…

Ask the children to tell you some of these 'feelings words' in a
<u>Hands up session.</u>
    Explore these words by talking about:
        what they mean
        where else you can use them
        those that mean the same
        those that mean the opposite.

I'm quarrelling with you because I don't like what you did. It doesn't mean I don't like you.

Explain that we all have these feelings from time to time but we must try to keep these feelings about what the child did and not about the child who did it.

<u>Further work</u>
Ask the children to draw a picture of two friends having a quarrel, and to write what the quarrel was about.

6. Making Up

Remind the children about the story of Jan and Del and the words they told about the feelings of people who quarrel..

Ask the children to tell you what they think Del and Jan could do to be friends again.

Pass the sentence
"Del could…

Pass the sentence
"Jan could…
(There will be a lot of repetition here, but in essence someone has to say they are sorry.)

Ask the children to think of ways to show that they are sorry.

Stand up if you can tell us one way.

> **You could show you are sorry by:**
>
> smiling at the person
> playing with them
> saying you won't do it again
> saying you didn't mean it
> asking how they feel
> asking them to play with you
> touching them gently
> being with them
> sharing your things
> thinking of them first.

Further work
Make a list of the ways children told you how we can show we are sorry and ask children to illustrate these. This could make a useful display which could be used when you need to help children to say they are sorry.

6. Making Up

Remind children about the story of Jan and Del. Tell the children just saying 'sorry' is not enough - they have to show that they mean it.

Ask them to put themselves in Jan's place and to think what Jan could do to show s/he is sorry.

Pass the sentence

"If I were Jan I would…

Share ideas

Ask the children to break into small groups of 4-5 and think of a time when someone said they were sorry - in a story or on TV perhaps? Give 2/3 minutes for discussion before re-forming the group/circle.

Ask one person from each small group to <u>tell the circle</u> what they have been talking about.

Further work

This could include discussion about blame and fault and how difficult it is to make up sometimes. Children could draw and write about Jan and Del making friends again, or about a time when they themselves ended a quarrel by making up.

After I quarrelled with my best friend we were both sad, so we made friends again. We said we would not be so silly another time.

31

7. Making others happy.

Tell the children that today they are going to be thinking about making others happy. Ask them to think for a minute about how they make their families, friends, teachers, pets or others happy.

<u>Pass the sentence</u>
"I make …. happy when I….

<u>Change places game.</u>
Stand up all the people who can think of someone

I make my kitten happy when I stroke her gently.

they made happy at home today. These children change places with one another.

Vary this by asking children to think of someone they made happy:
  in the school
   in the class
  on the way to school
  in the playground

<u>Further work</u>
This could include thinking of words that describe happy, drawings of people/pets they made happy
Work in PE/drama on this theme- 'How do you tell people are happy?' - show how these people look, feel, move.

7. Making others happy.

Ask children about how they can make their friends happy.

Go round the circle and ask children to tell one thing they can do that makes someone happy.

<u>Pass the sentence</u>

"I can ... to make someone happy.

Jot down what the children say to use later in the 'change places' game.

When all the children have had the opportunity to tell you, use the words from your list and ask children to stand up and change places.

<u>Stand up and change places</u>

if you said, for example:

you played with your friend

you talked to your friend

you listened to your friend

you comforted your friend etc.

<u>Further work</u>

You could ask the children to draw a picture of themselves in a circle and write around their picture names of people they made happy this week. Some children could write more about what they did to make these people happy.

Tidied up for Mrs Jones

Laid the table for Mum

Helped with my little sister

This is me

Let Sam go first

Shared crayons with Jim

Picked up the bricks

Waited my turn

Read a story with Rosie

8 When friends move - separation

Sometimes good friends move away and new ones come.
Ask the children to think of how they felt when someone
they loved moved away.
Relate this to a child or grown-up in the class or school who left.

I felt sad when Mrs Rhamm left.

<u>Pass the sentence</u>

"When… left I felt…"
Jot down the words they use – there will be many repetitions.
Children who repeat change places with the first person who
said the word.

<u>Pass the face</u>

Ask the children to show the person next to them how these feelings look. (If children find
this difficult say, for example, 'How do you look when you are sad/miserable/ angry/ worried/
missing them?')

They might feel: sad missing me; excited;
worried; looking forward; looking back;
angry; miserable....

When all have had their turn, ask them to
<u>Stand and tell</u>

if they can think of how the person moving felt. Can they give you words for this?
You could collect and display these words.

<u>Further work</u>

Talk to the children about keeping in touch with old friends.
Ask them how they can do this. Ask them to draw themselves
keeping in touch with someone who moved away and about
how they felt when they met them again.
Read *"A new home for Tiger"* by Joan Stimson (Scholastic, 1997).
It is in most school libraries

I am sending an e-mail to Rosie.

I miss you

8. When friends move - separation

(Sensitivity warning – You will know your children and when to do this activity. Be sensitive to feelings of anyone who has suffered a bereavement.)

With children focus on ways to remember people who move on. In some families a parent, older sibling, grandparent or pet may have moved away/left their family/died.

Ask the children to show by their face how they feel when someone or a pet moves away. <u>Pass the face</u> around the circle or group.

Now read a story to the children about someone who has gone away or died. – "Badger's Parting Gifts" by S. Varley, published by Picture Lions or "Grandma's Bill" by M Waddell published by Simon & Schuster) are in most school libraries.

<u>Pass the sentence</u>
"The person left behind felt…"

<u>Pass the sentence</u>
"When someone goes away you can remember them by…"

<u>Further work</u>
This could include making a list of things you could do to help you to keep in touch with someone who has gone away or ways to remember a pet or a person who has died.

Read *"I'll always love you"* by Hans Wilhelm (Hodder 1986) or *"Don't Forget to Write"* by Martin Selway, (Red Fox 1993). They are in most school libraries.

To remember people you can:

- think about how they looked,
- keep a picture
- keep a letter
- think of what they did
- remember things you did together
- talk about them
- remember things they told you.

---

1. When I was very young

Talk to the children about how they are growing up all the time – you can't see that you're growing, but every day they grow a tiny bit more.

Ask the children to think of things they could do when they were very young.
Pass the sentence
"When I was very young I could…"
Jot down what they say.

> When I was younger I could… cry, drink milk, crawl, sit up, sleep, go in a pram.

Play the change places game:
>   when a child repeats a word already given
>   wait until the end and ask those who said a certain word to stand up then change places.

Pass the face
Ask the children to think of how they feel when the see a very young baby. Pass this face around the circle.

Ask the children to tell you some of the nursery rhymes they learned when they were younger – can any of the children sing one to the group?

Further work
Children can bring in photos of themselves as babies (and as they are now) and you could display these with labels and comments from the children.
Collect picture books from the library to read to the children and display – such as *"The Trouble with Babies"*, by Angie & Chris Sage, published by Puffin 1991 and *"Aren't you lucky?"* by G. Anholt published by Red Fox 1991.

1. When I was very young

Remind children that we all started out as tiny babies and ask them to think of what babies need to grow healthy and happy.

<u>Pass the sentence</u>
  "I think a baby needs…"
  Jot down what they say -there will be some repetition

When everyone has had a turn read out what the children have told you.
Ask the children to stand and tell if they have missed anything out and if they still miss out some of the important things you can talk about these. (e.g. love, a loving home, grown-ups to take care of them, time to play)

I think a baby needs…
milk to drink
someone to care for them
clothes
a pram
a bed
somewhere quiet to sleep
toys
someone to play with them
love
a loving home
people who care.

Look again at your list and ask the children to help you to think which are the five most important things. Write these down on separate cards or paper.

<u>Choose</u>
  Place the cards around the room and ask the children to decide which they think is the most important. Ask them to go and stand by their choice.

<u>Further work</u>
  This can include counting the number of 'votes' to make a chart or asking the children to draw, write about and give reasons for their choice.
  This could make an interesting display with the chart as centrepiece surrounded by the children's writing/drawings, together with a piece of paper explaining what they did to find out this data.

2. Now I am (age) I can...

Tell the children about some of the things you can do now that you couldn't do when you were their age. Ask them to think of something they couldn't do when they were very young, but can do now.

<u>Pass the sentence</u>
"When I was very young I couldn't... but I can now.
Jot down each new thing they say.
Children who repeat change places with the last person who said it.

Now ask the children to think of something they have just learned to do.

<u>Stand, tell and sit down quickly</u>
Ask the children to do this quickly, telling everyone
something else that they can do now.
If the children are quick at doing this, there will
be a wave effect that ripples around the circle.
(You may need to practise this.)

When I was very young I couldn't...
walk, stand, run, eat, drink from a cup, talk, sing, think.

but I can now

<u>Further work</u>
Ask the children if they know any stories or poems about children growing up. Make a collection, read and display such books from the library. Include, if you can, *"Henry's baby"*, by M. Hoffman, (Dorling Kindersly 1993) and *"Hasn't he Grown"* by John Talbot (Andersen Press 1989).

2. Now I am (age) I can...

Ask children to think of what they can do now that is better than the things they did when they were younger.

<u>Pass the sentence</u>
"Now I am 6 (or 7) I can..."
Children who repeat a word change places with the
last person who said it.
Jot down what the children say.

<u>Stand, tell and sit down quickly.</u>
Ask the children to think of some skill they would like to
learn when they are older. Try to say it with very few words.

Ask children to <u>stand up if</u> they like being the age they are
now, rather than being younger.
Count how many.
Ask the children to work out how many would rather be younger.

Now we are in this class we can:

help younger children
show visitors around
school
do better drawings
read harder books
make interesting things
with junk.

We all like it better now
we are this age.

<u>Further work</u>
This could include making a display of what the children said.
Or ask the children to fold a piece of paper in half and head the two sides "What I could do when I was 5." "What I can do now I am 6 (7)" and draw pictures with labels or writing.

3. Looking back

Ask the children to think of some of the things they told you they used to do when they were young. Tell them that some of these things would have been happy but that some might have been sad.

Ask them all to think of one really happy thing they can remember that happened when they were younger.

<u>Pass the sentence</u>
"I remember being very happy when…"

When all the children have had their turn tell the children to show by their face how they felt.
<u>Pass the face</u> with that expression round the circle.

> I remember being very happy when my baby sister was born.

Now ask the children to think of some sad thing that they remember happening when they were very young.
<u>Stand up if</u> you can remember something sad from long ago.
Ask these children to think of a word to tell how they felt before they sit down.

<u>Further work</u>
Children can choose to draw pictures about a very happy or sad memory.
You could display these under the heading "Memories".

3. Looking back

Remind children of the Circle Time when they thought of things they could do when they were younger.

Ask the children to think of their memories.

> <u>Touch your nose if</u> you can think of a really sad memory.
> <u>Touch your head if</u> you can think of a really worrying memory.
> <u>Touch your toes if</u> you can think of a frightening memory.
> <u>Touch your chin if</u> you can think of a very funny memory.

Now ask them to think of a really special time when they were younger. It may have been a holiday, a birthday, Christmas or another special day, perhaps when they achieved something.

<u>Pass the sentence</u>

"My really special day was…"

Ask the children to turn to a partner, work in pairs, and to think of any memory and make their face show how they felt.
Ask their partner to guess how they felt and then tell them if they were right and what the happening was.

Back in the group/circle ask those children who guessed what feelings the face showed to stand up.

My really special memory is when my brother learned to drive the car.

He took us all out for a drive without L plates.

<u>Further work</u>

Children could make a memory book with a page for each age, illustrating the highs and lows. A class project could include work on various memories.

41

4. It takes time to grow

Tell the children that some animals or creatures grow up very quickly, but that children take quite a long time. Draw on your experience of the animal world (or on previous work with the children) and talk about how quickly, for example, a bird or puppy grows up to be independent of its parents.

Ask the children to think of the things that other creatures have to learn to do before they are grown up.

<u>Pass the sentence</u>
"…. have to learn to…"

Jot down what the children say and use this to make lists of what various animals have to learn before they are grown up.

Ask the children if they know how old they have to be before they can do certain things, for example:

Birds have to learn to:

eat
fly
find food
make nests.

Kittens have to learn to:

open their eyes
drink milk
eat
purr
run
find food
wash themselves.

Kittens grow into cats quickly.

<u>Touch your ears if</u> you know how old you must be to go swimming on your own.
<u>Touch your chin if</u> you know how old you must be before you can go to work.
<u>Touch your elbows if</u> you know how old you must be before you can marry.

<u>Further work</u>
Collect pictures of animal families with their young, pictures of people at various ages. These can be mounted with the message that baby animals grow quickly into adult animals but that human babies take a long time to grow into adults.

4. It takes time to grow

Ask children to think of how animals, birds and other creatures grow and what they have to learn to do before they leave parents and look after themselves.

Go round the group/circle asking each child to tell what various animals have to learn to do. e.g. "Puppies have to learn to dig," "Birds have to learn to fly."

When all children have had their turn ask all to stand up.

<u>Play the Stand up/count/sit down game:</u>
i.e. all children stand, those who said "They have to learn to eat" raise a hand. All count them (you write down the number) and these children sit down.

Choose different sentences until all children are sitting. This data would make a good display; add children's pictures or pictures from magazines.

This is what we think animals and birds have to learn.

4 of us said birds have to learn 'to fly'
3 of us said 'birds have to find their own food'
3 of us said ' birds have to make nests'
7 of us said 'dogs learn to run and jump'
8 of us said ' cats learn to wash their fur'
5 of us said 'dogs learn to eat bones.'

Animals and birds grow up quickly.

<u>Further work</u>
Ask children to draw and write about all the things a human child has to learn to do for itself before it is grown-up.
Link this work with sex education, making sure that the children know that:
it takes a man and a woman to make and have a baby
boys grow up into men who can help to make babies
girls grow into women who can have their own babies
there is a lot to learn before they can do that.

43

5. I know I'm getting bigger because…

Remind the children that they were babies once and are not babies any more – what happened? Talk to the children about growing bigger.

<u>Pass the sentence</u>

"I know (I am getting bigger) because…"
Children who repeat a response can **change places** with the last person who said that.
Ask them to tell you something that they can do now that they are bigger and are in school.

<u>Pass the sentence</u>

"Now I am at school I can…
Jot down appropriate or interesting responses.

Ask the children to think about whether being older is better than being younger.
Tell the children to say 'yes' or 'no' and to:
<u>Stand and tell</u> and sit down quickly.

<u>Further work</u>

Ask the children to draw what they have told you. Display their pictures surrounded by some of the responses you jotted down.
Remind the children that it takes a long time and there is a lot to learn before children are grown up.

5. I know I'm getting bigger because…

Tell children that we know they are growing bigger because they need larger clothes and are changing physically –new teeth, long bones etc.

Ask them to think of other ways they know they are growing up.
What can they do now that they couldn't do before?
What are they now allowed to do?

Now I am older I can…

wash myself
put myself to bed
ride my bike
lay the table
run faster
reach things.

<u>Answer and question</u>
"Now I'm growing up I'm allowed to … what are you allowed to do?

Play the change places game if children repeat what has been said.
Jot down what the children say and when all have had a turn choose and read out six items from your list. Write them up somewhere for all to see.

Now ask the children to think which is the most important of these six things they are now allowed to do.

<u>Choose</u>
Ask all children to stand.
When you read out their choice, they go to the front
(or the middle if you have a circle) and count themselves
before going back to sit down.
Write the number alongside each word to decide which the majority chose.

I'm allowed
to stay up
late on
Saturdays.

<u>Further work</u>
Ask the children to record, illustrate and display this data.

6. Who helps us to grow and learn?

Ask the children to think about how they managed to learn all these new things that have helped them to grow and learn.

<u>Start the sentence</u>
"…. helps me to grow and learn."
There will be many repetitions but jot down what the children say, putting a tick for repeats. (All responses are correct - children will say words such as "food" as well as people's names.)

When all the children have had their turn read out your list and tell the children how many of them gave that same answer.

Select the four most mentioned people from your list, write them up on flipchart or chalk board and ask the children to think about what these people do to help them to grow and learn.

Ask children to choose which person they tell about.

<u>Stand and tell</u>
" … helps me to…"

<u>Further work</u>
Children can draw a picture of their person and you can help them to write a label or caption about their drawing.

My sister helps me to read my book.

Mum helps me to get dressed.

Dad helps me to ride my bike.

6. Who helps us to grow and learn?

Ask children to think of all the people who are helping them to grow and learn new things.

Start a <u>question and answer game </u>which can go round the circle.
"Who is helping you to grow and learn new things?"
"My sister is helping me. Who is helping you?"
There will be some repetition, they may need help - remind them of out of school activities such as swimming, football, sewing, cooking, clubs.

<u>Can you guess?</u>
Ask for volunteers to mime what someone is helping them to do.
Children who think they can guess stand up.
The child miming can select children to answer until
someone says the correct answer.

<u>Further work</u>
Ask children to work in small groups and with each choosing a different adult outside the home who helps people.
Ask them each to illustrate and write about what their chosen person does.
Mount these together to make a group display.

The swimming instructor is helping me to learn to swim.

Like this

7. New responsibilities

Ask the children to think about things they now do at home or at school which show that they are growing up. Tell the children that they will enjoy doing some of these things but that there may be things they don't like doing. Jot down what the children say for later discussion.

<u>Pass the sentence</u>
"I am growing up. I like to…"

Play the <u>change places game</u> when children repeat someone's answer.

Finish with an <u>active session:</u>
    If you like being more grown up -stand up
    If you like helping at home - curl up small
    If you like tidying up – clap once
    If you can dress yourself – touch your nose.

    Add other new responsibilities with activities such as
    wave your hand,   touch your knee,
    stand on one leg,   hop once.

> We like doing these things now we are growing up:
>
> going to bed later
> choosing what we eat
> helping in the kitchen
> playing out with friends
> watching TV later
> choosing new clothes
> helping with the baby
> help with shopping
> choose things.

<u>Further work</u>
Discuss what the children said in the first part of this activity. Can they group things into things they like doing very much and things they don't much like doing.

Ask the children to find pictures of children helping. They can tear or cut these out to make a collage picture – 'Children are growing up'. Add your own questions in speech bubbles such as 'Who is helping to cook?' 'Can you do some of these things?' 'What can you do to help?'

7. New responsibilities

Before Circle Time ask the children to draw two picture of themselves doing:
- one new thing that they <u>like doing to help</u> now they are growing up
- one new thing they <u>have to do</u> – but may not like doing very much.

Ask the children to bring their pictures to the group/circle to remind them what they are going to say.

<u>Pass the sentence</u>

"I like doing… but I don't like doing…"

Jot down the things that the children do like doing so that you can talk about these when all children have finished.

Ask children to think whether they like having these new responsibilities.

Ask them to say yes or no, when they...

<u>Stand and tell</u> and sit down quickly

Talk to the children about new responsibilities they will have as they are growing up and how there will be more of these as they grow and move through school.

Things we can do to help now we are growing up.

tidying up
helping to lay the table
putting our clothes away
remembering messages
answering the phone
working in the garden
reading to my little brother.

<u>Further work</u>

Make an interesting display using the children's pictures.

Write alongside in large speech bubbles some of the things they said.

8. Looking Forward

Is there something that you are learning (and are looking forward to being able to do) that you could tell the children about?

Ask the children to think of some of the things that children in the next class (or that they in a year's time) can do.

Ask them to think of one thing that they are looking forward to being able to do.

Can any of them can show what this skill/activity is?

Stand and mime

Children can do this at the front (or in the middle of the circle) – perhaps several at the same time. Ask those watching in the circle to guess what the children are doing.

Pass the sentence

"When I am (5/6/in next class) I will be able to…
Chose 4 or 5 of these new skills/activities.
Write them up on separate cards or paper.

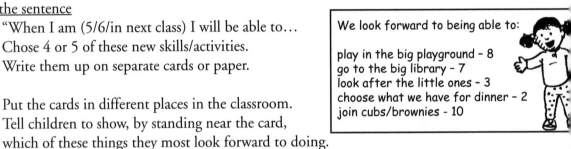

We look forward to being able to:

play in the big playground – 8
go to the big library – 7
look after the little ones – 3
choose what we have for dinner – 2
join cubs/brownies – 10

Put the cards in different places in the classroom.
Tell children to show, by standing near the card,
which of these things they most look forward to doing.
Ask each group to count its members and note down the number against the skill/activity.

Further work

Make a display of the children's choices, by pinning up the cards with the number of children who chose it. Ask the children to write their names to put alongside the chosen activity. Add a title such as "We want to learn to do these."

Ask children to think about and draw themselves doing something that they would like to do/ be when they are fully grown up.

8. Looking Forward

Ask children to think of what skills they look forward to being able to master. Talk about physical skills – e.g. cycle riding, swimming, skipping, academic skills – reading, maths, writing and co-operative skills e.g. taking responsibility for self/others/possessions. Remind the children that growing up includes all three of these areas.

Draw three boxes on the flipchart/ board and label them 'skills', 'learning', 'responsibility'.

Pass the sentence

"I look forward to the time when I ..."
As each child finishes the sentence ask the group to decide which box it fits into.

Either write the words or make a mark in the relevant box. When all the children have had their turn ask them to decide which of the three areas of growing-up they think is the most import

Play the <u>Stand up/hands up/count/sit down game</u> to collect this data. (see Growing up 4, older infants).

> I look forward to being able to swim. This will be a new skill.

> I look forward to learning about the Greeks. This will be learning.

> I look forward to the time when I can go out at night with my friends. This will be a responsibility.

Further work

Children can make individual "We are growing up" books or draw pictures of themselves doing the activity they most look forward to being able to do to make a class display.

Make a display using three overlapping circles with three headings, skills, learning, responsibilities. Add pictures and quotes from children in the appropriate circle. (If some fit into more than one circle use the space where circles overlap.)

Read *"Leaving Mrs. Ellis"* by Catherine Robinson (Red Fox 1997).
It is in most school libraries.

1. Feeling good

Tell the children that today you want them to think about when they feel really good and happy. Tell them to show by their face how they feel when they are feeling good and happy.
<u>Pass the face around the circle</u>
Now ask them to think of some of the things that make them feel really good.

<u>Pass the sentence</u>
"I feel really good when…"
Jot down the key words of what they say; when all have had their turn read out your list.
You may find that the responses can be put into several categories such as 'something I have' e.g. a present or toy, 'something I have done' e.g. an achievement such as finishing a book, 'something someone has done for/to me'.
Talk about the different kinds of things that make us feel good.
Now ask the children to think of something they can do to make someone in their family feel good. Ask them to say that person's name. Stand <u>up/tell /sit down.</u>

Now ask the children to think about how they themselves
feel when they have done something to make someone else feel good.

We feel
happy
good
glad
lovely
pleased.

<u>Pass the sentence.</u>
"When I make someone else feel good it makes me feel…"
Jot down these 'feelings' words e.g. happy, glad, surprised, pleased, excited. Very young children may only used the words you gave – happy, good. Write up the words they tell you and, when all have had their turn, ask if they can think of any other words to add.

<u>Further work</u>
Children can draw themselves making someone else feel good. Label their drawings or use speech bubbles to show what they are saying.

1. Feeling good

Ask children to think of something they have done recently that made them feel good about themselves.

Ask them to show the kind of face they have when they are feeling good.

<u>Pass the face round the circle</u>

Ask the children to think of a word/phrase that they could use instead of 'feeling good'.

Children who repeat change places with the last person who said the word.

Jot these words down and after all children have had a turn read out your list.

Ask the children to tell one thing that make them feel good about themselves.

<u>Pass the sentence</u>
"I feel good when …"

Ask the children to think of something they could do
to make someone at school feel good today, and tell what
they could do. (Ask them not to say anyone's name.)

<u>Pass the sentence</u>
"To make someone feel good I could…."

Feeling good words
happy, good glad, lovely friendly, thoughtful helped, kindly caring, excited better, loving wonderful.

<u>Further work</u>

Ask children to put the list of words in some kind of order – alphabetical or families.

Make a chart of the words with children's pictures alongside each word.

Ask children to choose one word to illustrate and write about.

Group work – ask a group to write about something that made their group feel good.

2. Feelings we share

Ask the children to think of times when they are not feeling good and how they look then.
Ask them to make that face and show the people sitting near.
Ask the children to think about something that feels not good.

<u>Make the face, Pass the sentence</u>
"This is how I felt when…

Feelings we share
We told about feeling sad (10)
We old about feeling worried (3)
We told about feeling scared (6)

If you can – suggest the word that would name that feeling and say
it to the group e.g. "So you felt worried when you dropped the glass".

When all the children have had their turn go over the feelings the children told about - and perhaps list them on the chalk board.

<u>Stand up</u> Ask the children to stand up if they shared the same feelings, e.g. "If you told me that you felt sad (or silly, worried or scared), stand up.
Ask the children to help to count the number of standing children and add the number to the list you made.

Remind the children that we all have these feelings from time
to time – we need to recognise these feelings in other people so
that we can know how they are feeling.

<u>Further work</u>
Show the children how to make faces show expression
by the shape of the mouth or eyes. Ask them to draw faces
to show different expressions.
Label these faces – perhaps grouping them together to make a class collage.
List the feelings words and use for reading practice or spelling aids.

2. Feelings we share

<u>Tell children this simple story</u>

Sam was trying hard to help his mum to tidy the table. There was a puzzle on the table which Sam's brother Tom had nearly finished. Sam carried the box with the puzzle very carefully but he didn't notice the kitten was near his feet. Just as he got to the table, he tripped over the kitten and fell over. Sam's fingers were hurting where they hit the table and the puzzle was spoilt.

Ask the children to think about how the people in the story felt.

<u>Make a face and say it</u>

Ask them to choose Sam, Tom or Mum, make the appropriate face and say how they felt.
"I think … 's face would like this. They would feel…"

Ask for volunteers to show and tell how they think:
Mum would have looked and felt if she had spoiled the puzzle,
Tom would have looked and felt if he had spoilt the puzzle himself.

Talk to the children about the importance of recognising how other people are feeling.
Can they tell you what they could do to help people to feel better?

I think the kitten would have looked like this.

<u>Stand and tell</u>

"To make someone feel better you could…"

<u>Further work</u>

Ask the children to think of a time when they hurt someone's feelings by accident. Ask them to draw a picture and write a sentence about it.

Older children could write about how they felt when this happened and what they did to try to make it better.

3. How can we tell how people are feeling?

Ask the group to think about this story:

"Chris was playing with friends in the playground. Sanjay knocked Chris down. Chris sat there for a minute trying to think how it felt. Sally came and helped Chris up but Anwar thought Chris looked funny sitting there and began to laugh."

Ask the children to think about how Chris, Sanjay, Sally and Anwar were feeling. Ask how we could tell how they were feeling.

Ask them to show by their face/body how each child might have felt.

Divide the group/circle into four parts and ask the children in the first part to pretend they were Chris and show everyone how he would have felt.

<u>Look and say</u>

"I think Chris would have looked and felt like this."
Ask the next quarter of children to think of Sanjay and so on until all the children have had their turn.

<u>Stand up</u>

if you have fallen over and people have laughed at you,
if you have laughed at someone when they got hurt.

<u>Standing and showing</u>

Ask for a volunteer to stand up and be one of the children in the story to show (mime) how that person felt. Ask the other children to put up hands if they can guess who the person is. The person who guesses can be the next to have a turn.

<u>Further work</u>

Ask children to draw a picture of the story (or of one of the children) and say what happened next. Put their words in a speech bubble.

3. How can we tell how people are feeling?

Ask children to think about how people show how they feel. Explain that we show our feelings not only by our face but also by our body language.

Demonstrate to the children how body and face can look when feeling sad, happy, excited.

<u>Pass the face/body</u>

Play this game around the group/circle, with children standing up to show by faces and bodies emotions such as: joy, excitement, fear, worry, happiness, love, wonder.

(The teacher can choose the feeling or ask children to choose and say which feelings they are showing.)

Read the story of Chris, Sanjay, Sally and
Anwar from the younger children's section.

Go round a quarter of the circle with question 1.
Vary the name so that all 4 children's feelings are explored.
(The second format may be easier for some children.)
1. "How do you think Chris felt?" "What made you think that?"
2. "I think Chris (or Sanjay/Sally/Anwar) felt… because s/he was…"

<u>Further work</u>

Tell the children that we call these feelings emotions. Perhaps they can list one feeling and draw how people look when they feel like that.

Ask older children to   * choose one of the characters in the story
                       * draw that character
                       * think of what could have happened next
                       * write a good ending.

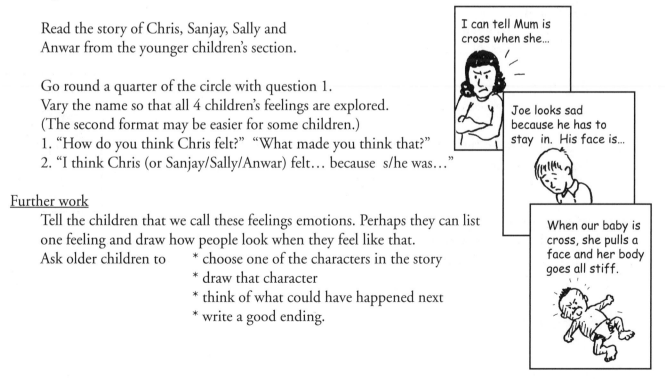

I can tell Mum is cross when she…

Joe looks sad because he has to stay in. His face is…

When our baby is cross, she pulls a face and her body goes all stiff.

4. Feelings change

I am sad.

Ask the children to think about how people are all the same.
<u>Stand up if...</u>
>   Ask the children to stand up if they have:
>   two eyes, hair, two legs, (choosing attributes that all children possess)

<u>Stand up if…</u>
>   Ask the children to stand up if they have:
>   blue eyes, long/short hair, black/brown hair, (choosing attributes that are fairly constant).

<u>Stand up if…</u>
>   Ask the children to stand up if they have:
>   Black shoes, blue cardigans, white socks, green jerseys (choosing attributes that change).

<u>Pass the sentence</u>
>   "I'm the same as you because I have… (blue eyes, two ears, brown hair)"

Now ask the children to think of how their feelings change.
<u>Pass the sentence</u>
>   "Yesterday I felt… but today I feel…"

I am not sad.

<u>Further work</u>
>   Ask the children to draw two pictures of themselves – one where they are happy and one
where they are not happy. Talk to the children about their pictures as you label them.

4. Feelings change

Ask children to think of some time when they felt bad, sad, unhappy or miserable and what happened or what they did to make themselves feel better.

<u>Pass the sentence</u>
"When I feel sad, I…"
Jot down what the children say and when all have had their turn discuss ways to make ourselves feel better.

Ask the children to tell you some of these 'feelings words' in a hands up session.

Explore these words by talking about:
• what they mean
• where else you can use them
• those that mean the same (e.g. nervous / frightened)
• those that mean the opposite. (e.g. happy / sad)
Could some of the children use these words in other sentences?
Ask the children to think of the feelings of their friends and families.
What can they do to help when these people feel sad or unhappy?

<u>Pass the sentence</u>
"When… feels sad I can make them feel better by/if/when…"

<u>Further work</u>
Ask children to draw themselves on some occasion when they felt unhappy and help them to write what made them feel better.
Make a collage of speech bubbles with advice to people who feel bad.

<u>Making me feel better.</u>
When Jim feels bad, he goes to read a book.
When Sara feels miserable she watches TV.
When Jo feels unhappy he goes out to play football.

<u>Helping others to feel better.</u>
You can…
tell them a joke
say you understand
play with them
take them out somewhere
give them a hug
ask them to choose what to do.

I know you feel bad now, but let's have a game of football to cheer you up.

You'll feel better tomorrow. Remember I'm your friend - come to my house and we'll play together.

5. Feeling afraid- what can we do?

Tell the children of some occasion when you yourself felt afraid - noises in the dark, when you were alone - and what you did to overcome this fear.

Choose each of the following in turn and ask children to:

Stand up

if you are afraid of the dark/ fireworks/loud bangs etc.

Ask the children to think of what they do when they are afraid.

Pass the sentence

"When I'm scared I…"

Reassure children that it is natural to feel afraid sometimes, and that this often helps us to take care of ourselves. (If there is something that you know your class is afraid of, perhaps you can talk about that here.)

Choose one or more of the following to pass round the circle.

Pass the sentence

"If you are afraid of the dark you can…" "If you are afraid of TV you can…"

"If you are afraid of blood you can…" "If you are afraid of a person you can…"

When children express their fears they find that many of them have the same fears - this alone can give confidence to overcome them.

Further work

Look in the library for picture books to read about overcoming fears - such as:

"A Lion at Bedtime" by Debi Gliori, ISBN 0-590-54111-0

"Janine and the Carnival" by Iolette Thomas, ISBN 0-233-98090-3

"Oliver and the Monsters" by Tony Blundell, ISBN 0-670-83842-X

"Dog Dottington" by Diana Hendry, ISBN 0-7445-3284-1

5. Feeling afraid - what can we do?

Ask children to do a piece of drawing and writing before they come to the circle. Tell them you want them to draw someone who is afraid and to write what they are afraid of.

<u>Show and tell</u>
Children show and tell about their picture. After all have had their turn ask if their fears fit into any categories. They may suggest fears that are real, fears that involve their own wrongdoing and fears that are fantasy and unlikely to happen.

<u>Real fears</u>	<u>Doing wrong fears</u>	<u>Fantasy fears</u>
falling out of bed	getting found out after:	things in the dark
getting into trouble	taking things	getting beamed up by aliens
breaking things	going to places out of bounds	swimming in shark filled waters
people being cross.	doing things they shouldn't.	getting hit by lightening.

Ask the children which fears are the most important to overcome.
Look at some of the examples the children gave and ask for solutions to these problems.

<u>Show by your face</u>
    1. how your feel when afraid,
    2. how you feel when your fear goes away.

This is Sofie. She is afraid of monsters under the bed.

<u>Further work</u>
    Ask children to write alongside or on the back of their pictures
    some ways for the person they drew to overcome their fear.
    Read some stories about overcoming fear – look at the suggestions for younger children.

6. Good Persuasion

Ask the children to tell you what they think persuasion is. With youngest children you may have to give them the word and explain what it means. (To persuade someone is to make them do something you want them to do, e.g. Please tidy up/clean your teeth/ put your coat on/watch the baby.)

Good persuaders want us to:
pick up rubbish
keep things nice
help them
play with them
share things
lend things.

<u>Pass the sentence</u>
> Choose one or both
> "Good persuasion is when you persuade us to…
> "It's good when you/Mum/Dad/My family persuades me to…

> Talk about how people look and talk when they try to persuade us to do something. Who persuades us?

<u>Pass the sentence</u>
> ".… persuades us to…

<u>Pass the face</u>
> Pretend someone wants to persuade you to play their game. How will they look?

Good persuaders ask us:
with a smile
in a nice voice
quietly
politely.

<u>Stand up and tell.</u>
> Pretend they want to persuade you to do something. What will they say, how will they say it?

<u>Further work</u>
> Ask children to draw a grown up at school persuading them to do something.

6. Good Persuasion

Ask children to think of a time when someone persuaded them to do something good for someone else (e.g. write a letter, make a gift, tidy the garden, help to wash the car).

Ask the children to think of how the persuader looked and what they said. How did they look?

<u>Pass the face</u>
What did they say and how did they say it? -use their voice.

<u>Pass the sentence</u>
They said, " ..."
Ask how they felt when they were persuaded.

<u>Pass the sentence</u>
"When I did what the person persuaded me to do, I felt..."

<u>Stand up and tell</u>
If you can think of times when people get together
to try to persuade others to do something good,
(e.g. clear up litter, give money for charity, petition
for a crossing, ask for help on a school/community project).

We brought tokens to school to help to buy computers.
We bought stickers to help to save the whale.
We sponsored an animal in the wildlife park.
We had a sponsored walk to raise money for charity.
People went to the council to ask for a crossing.

<u>Further work</u>
Ask children to work in groups to write a letter/make a poster to persuade people to either come to school to help or to give articles for a charity fundraising event. Help them with the choice of words they need to use.

7. Bad persuasion

Remind the children that there are two kinds of persuasion:
>when people ask you to do something that is good for you or others
>when people ask you to do something that is bad for you or others.

Ask the children to think of times when people have tried to persuade them to do something that is not right.

<u>Pass the sentence</u>
"Its not right when someone tries to persuade you to…

What kind of face does a bad persuader make?
What kind of voice does a bad persuader have?
<u>Show their face</u> and say in their voice:
"Come on, let's do it, no one will know"

It's OK

<u>Bad persuaders</u>
try to make you
say they'll hurt you if you don't
say they'll give you things if you do
try to force you
say no one will find out.

<u>Stand up, change places</u>
If someone has ever tried to persuade you to do something bad.
Tell the children they must always say 'NO' to a bad persuader.

<u>Further work</u>
Read or tell the story of Little Red Riding Hood. Talk to the children about the big bad wolf persuading her to do something that was bad for her. What should she have said to the wolf?

7. Bad persuasion

Remind children that there is both good and bad persuasion.

<u>Stand up, change places</u>

Ask children to stand up if someone has ever tried to persuade them to do something they know is wrong. They can change places with anyone standing up.

<u>Stand up, change places</u>

Ask children to stand up if someone has ever tried to persuade them to do something they know is dangerous. Change places.

Ask them to think of why people might want to persuade them to do something bad.

<u>Pass the sentence</u>

"They might want to persuade you to do something bad because...
Children who repeat change places with the person who said it last.

Jot down what the children say and when they have all had their turn talk about what they have said.

<u>Further work</u>

Talk about the consequences of being persuaded to do something wrong or dangerous. Ask the children whose fault it is if they are persuaded to do that.

(See the next page for ideas for helping children to say 'no'.)

Ask the children to write a story about someone who was tempted to do something they knew was wrong or dangerous.

<u>People might want to persuade you to do something bad because:</u>

it makes them feel good
they want to control you
they want you to do something they dare not do
they want you to share the blame.

8. Saying 'no' to bad persuasion

Remind the children that there is good persuasion as well as bad and that they should not be saying 'no' unless someone is trying to persuade them to do something wrong or dangerous.

<u>Stand up, change places</u>

Ask children to stand up if a friend has ever tried to persuade them to do something they know is wrong or dangerous. <u>Change places.</u>

Ask the children to think of what they should say if someone tries to persuade them to do something that is wrong or dangerous.

<u>Pass the sentence</u>

"You could say…"

Ask the children to think of what they should do if someone tries to persuade you to do something wrong or dangerous.

<u>Pass the sentence</u>

"You could…

No!

<u>Saying No</u>
No, I'm not going to.
No, it's wrong.
No, its not fair.
No, its dangerous.
No, that's silly.
No, that could hurt someone.

If young children give inappropriate responses to both the above, intervene - suggest better things to say and do. Jot down useful responses for later.

What we really want the children to say is 'No' and what we want them to do is to go away quickly from the person trying to persuade them.

<u>Stand up</u>

Ask those children who said 'say no' to stand up and ask them to say 'no' to the rest of the group.

<u>You could say</u>
No
Go away
I'll tell a grown-up
I'm not going to.

<u>Further work</u>

Practise saying no in a firm way. Repeat this sentence "No I'm not going to."

8. Saying 'no' to bad persuasion

Remind children that there are two kinds of persuasion and that they should always say 'no' to persuasion if it means doing or saying something wrong, dangerous or hurtful.

<u>Pass the sentence</u>
"Bad persuasion is when someone tries to make you…"
<u>Change places</u> if children repeat what has already been said.

Tell children that it is sometimes difficult to resist persuasion.
Tell them the best way is to start their sentence with 'No'.

Ask the children to think of one example from the 'pass the sentence' and to think of what they would say if someone tried to persuade them to do that.

NO!

Ways to say 'no'
Look them in the eye
Stand straight and tall
Take a deep breath
Start with 'no'
You don't need to give a
reason – just say
'it's wrong'
'it's dangerous'
'someone could get hurt.'

<u>Pass the sentence</u>
"No I won't, because…
Ask the children to think how they will say 'No' – How will it sound?
How will their face look? How will their body look?
Ask the children to <u>Stand and tell</u> ways to say 'No'. (Make sure they do this in a forceful way.)

Jot down anything appropriate that the children tell you about ways to say 'No' and include their responses in a chart for children to read and remember.

<u>Further work</u>
Use drama to explore ways of saying 'no' to a partner.
Ask children to choose one of the 'ways to say no' and to illustrate this.
Use some of their pictures to illustrate your chart.

1. Who am I?

Hill Top infants
phone 6237
27th J
43 Sout Stre
I am 5 and a half
Mrs Za next do
I am sam Jones

Tell the children that it is important to remember who they are, where they live and their phone number.

<u>Pass the question and answer</u>

Ask children to pass this question and answer round the circle.

Can they remember to say all their names? Start by saying your name to the first child.

"My name is … Who are you?

<u>Stand up and count</u>

Ask the children to stand up if they can remember where they live/their address.

Ask these children to count themselves.

(Start with one child saying 'one', the next says 'two' and so on until all have been counted.)

Ask all or select a few children to tell the group their address.

> We know who we are
> 15 of us know our names
> 6 of us remember our address
> 6 of us remember our phone number
> 20 of us remember the name of our school.

<u>Touch your ears</u> if you can remember your telephone number.

<u>Touch your nose</u> if you can remember your birthday.

<u>Put your elbows together</u> if you can remember the name of our school

<u>Put your hands round your back</u> if you can think of another safe house as well as where you live.

<u>Further work</u>

Ask children to draw themselves outside their house and write their name and address.

Ask them to draw themselves at their last birthday party, to draw the cake with candles and write their birth date.

1. Who am I?

Before Circle Time ask children to write their full name and draw their home with the correct colour front door. Ask them to draw all the people who live in their home.

Can they put the number/name on the door and write their address/phone number?

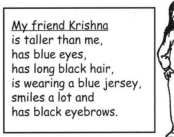

In Circle Time ask two or three children at a time to stand up and show their picture.

> We know all these safe places:
> Grandma's house
> The lady next door's house
> School
> Church
> Police Station
> Our shop.

Then ask all children to:
   hands up if they can say all their names
   stand up if they can say all their address
   wave one hand if they can say their phone number
   jump three times if they can tell you another safe place as well as their own home.

Pass the sentence. (Remind children that they can say "I don't know")
   "Another safe place is…"

Further work
   Ask them to draw a friend and write a description of them.
   They could describe (orally or in writing)
   a child who is out of sight,
   a teacher or other well known adult at school,
   a parent or member of their family.

> My friend Krishna
> is taller than me,
> has blue eyes,
> has long black hair,
> is wearing a blue jersey,
> smiles a lot and
> has black eyebrows.

69

2. Who keeps me safe?

Ask the children to think of people who keep them safe.

People who keep us safe.
our families
the police
the crossing patrol
our teachers
doctors
nurses
bus driver.

<u>Pass the answer and question</u>
    You can start by asking the nearest child:
    "... keeps me safe. Who keeps you safe?"

    Children who repeat a response change places with the child who said it last.
    Many children will name family members, so only list the category e.g 'parent'.

<u>Stand and tell</u>
    Name a person (e.g. police officer) from your list and ask the children to think of what this person does to keep us safe. Ask them to stand up in turn and show (mime) what the person does. (Change the person as you go round the circle so that you get through the list.)

<u>Pass the sentence</u>
    "My sister (friend/police officer/crossing patrol etc.) keeps me safe when…

<u>Further work</u>
    Ask children to draw one person who keeps us safe.
    Help them to write a label or sentence for their picture about how these people keep us safe. Children may want to take their pictures home - they could make a good classroom display.

2. Who keeps me safe?

Before Circle Time ask children to think of people who keep them safe and to work in groups of three or four to make a combined list.

At Circle Time ask one of each group to name the people they wrote.
Write these people's names (or jobs) on the chalkboard as each group read out their list.

When all children have had their turns, look down the list and ask each group to choose one person and think how they can show (i.e. act out) this person at work.
Send the small groups of children to different parts of the classroom to practise how they will do this – allow no more than 4 minutes.

Mime and guess

In turn ask each group to show their chosen person showing what they do to keep people safe.
Ask children from the circle to touch their nose when they think they have guessed the job.
Allow no more than 2 guesses before asking the actors to tell.

Further work

Arrange visits from people such as the school nurse, police, fire officers, road safety officers etc.
Ask children to work together to make a collage of people who help to keep us safe.
Ask children to work in pairs to write about and illustrate one person.

These people help to keep us safe.

Our families   the police   our teacher   the nurse   crossing patrol   child minder

3. I can keep myself safe

Tell the children that they have a job to – to help the people who keep them safe.

Ask them to think of all the things they can do to help the crossing patrol, police, families, teacher.

This is Shiulie keeping safe going shopping.

I am holding Mum's hand

<u>Pass the sentence</u> (choose one of these)

"I can help by…"

"I can help my teacher (grandma, etc.) to keep me safe by…"

<u>Stand and tell</u>

Ask the children to think of places where they play.

Now ask children to think about how they keep themselves safe in these locations. (You may need to add others, for example:

bedroom,	garden,	kitchen,	classroom,	playground,
park,	seaside,	forest,	street,	swimming pool.

Change the location in the sentence so that you get through the above list.

<u>Pass the sentence</u>

"I keep safe in my bedroom (my garden etc.) …"

<u>Further work</u>

Ask the children to draw themselves keeping safe in one of these places.

Ask them to tell you what they are doing.

Write what they say on their picture or in a speech bubble on a coloured piece of paper alongside so that everyone can read it.

3. I can keep myself safe

Remind children that they have an important part to play in keeping themselves safe.

<u>Stand up, change places</u>
> Ask the children to stand up/change places if they can:
>> remember doing something that kept them safe
>> remember doing something that didn't keep them safe
>> remember doing something that hurt someone else.
> Ask them to think of one thing they can do to keep safe.

I remember walking along a high wall and I fell off.
This was doing something that didn't keep me safe.

<u>Pass the sentence</u>
> "I can… to keep myself safe."

<u>Tell the children this story:</u>
> *Azif was leaning out of a car window without a seat belt on as it drove down the High Street. Alice and Paco had a little dog and wanted to cross the road to go to the shop. Ben had his ball on the ground and was kicking it about as he walked to the park. Jo thought he would cross the road between some parked cars.*

<u>Share ideas</u>
> Divide the group/circle into five parts and ask each part what they would say to one of the children.
> Give the children a few minutes to discuss this in their groups.

I would tell Azif to close the car window and put his seat belt on..

<u>Stand and tell</u>
> "I would tell Azif…"I would tell Alice…"I would tell Paco…etc.

<u>Further work</u>
> Explore this scenario in role play in drama sessions.
> Ask children to re-write the story with the children all keeping themselves safe.

4. At home.

Tell the children that they their home is a safe place but they must still take care not to do anything that could hurt themselves or other people. Ask the children to think of where they play inside their homes.

> We can play
> in the sitting room
> in the hall
> in the kitchen
> in the bedroom
> in the dining room
> on the stairs.

Pass the sentence

"I play in …

There will be many repetitions, but jot down each room the children mention.

Make a list of these rooms on the chalkboard and ask the children to think about which are the safest places inside their homes to play.

Stand up/sit down

Stand up if you think the kitchen (your bedroom/sitting room/hallway/ stairs etc.) is the safest place. Jot down the numbers of children who stand up for each room.

When you have gone through all the rooms on your list, ask the children which room they now think is the very safest place to play in their house.

Stand up and count

Go through the list again this time asking children to stand up when you say the place they think is the least safe place to play in their homes.

Will they say the stairs? Talk about how it can be unsafe to play on the stairs.

Further work

Ask the children to draw themselves playing in a safe place in their home.

Or make a large picture of the inside of a house, showing all the rooms, ask (or help) children to draw and cut out a picture of themselves to place in the safe rooms.

Write 'safety' questions on large speech bubbles "Is it good to play here?"

4. At home

Ask children to think of their own homes and to think of safe things which could be dangerous if they were not used properly. Give an example – a pair of scissors is a safe thing use to cut something carefully, but not to stick into someone.

Ask the children to work in pairs or fours and to make a quick list of things which are really safe if used carefully but could be harmful if not used correctly.
Allow 2 minutes for this.

<u>Tell one new thing</u>
Ask each group to tell everyone one thing from their list that has not already been said and cross off things as they are mentioned. You could write these up.

When all children have had their turn ask children to <u>stand and tell</u> if they still have something on their list.

<u>What would you say?</u>
Ask for volunteers to tell the group what they would say to someone who was using one of these objects in an unsafe way.
"I would say…"

<u>Further work</u>
Ask children to write a list of advice about using things safely in their homes.

<u>Keep yourself safe</u>

Keep scissors closed in your hand.
Don't walk about with a knife.
Keep away from electric plugs.
Use things in the proper way.
Anything could be unsafe if not used properly.
Keep away from hot things.

5. Outside

Tell the children that there are safe and unsafe places to play outside. Can they think of the safe places?

Don't go too near the BBQ. It's hot.

<u>Stand and tell</u>
"A safe place to play is…

<u>Change places</u> for repeats.

<u>Stand and tell</u>
Ask children to tell you where they go.
Jot down a list – e.g. seaside, park, riverside, a theme park/zoo, picnics, BBQs.
Include other local places.

<u>Pass the sentence</u>
"At a BBQ you keep safe by…"
Change the location after three or four children have answered.
Jot down any appropriate responses.

Before the end of the session use your jotted list to remind the children of what they have told you. You could use items from your list to make a display.

<u>Further work</u>
Ask the children to draw some of the places where they go. Write their keeping safe message on their picture.

5. Outside

Remind children that even in safe places there can be dangers.
Ask children to tell of what could be unsafe in their garden (on the road/playground/park/seaside).

Pass the sentence
"It could be unsafe in/at ... if you …"

Jot down some of the dangers they tell you on separate cards or papers. When all children have had their turn read out what you have written – e.g. - hot things, ponds, rivers, high places, railways, building site, bridges etc.

Spread the cards around the classroom and tell children to stand near the card of their choice to show which of these things they think is the most dangerous.
Ask each group to count its members and note down the total against the danger.

Now ask one child from each group to hold the card with the rest of their group behind them to make a 'living chart'.

Further work
You could make a permanent chart of this data yourself or ask children to make a 'pictorial representation' by drawing their face to put in their choice of column on a chart.
 Label the display and explain what the data shows.
Ask children to draw and write about how they kept safe in one of these locations.

6. Keeping my body healthy and safe

Ask the children to <u>stand and tell</u> if they know what 'healthy' means. Jot down responses from these children and discuss them. Because 'healthy' is a difficult concept, you may need to help them to understand that 'healthy' means growing fit, strong and well and keeping themselves safe.

Ask the children to tell you what they can do to make themselves healthy and fit and well.

To keep your body healthy you can

eat good food
run about
play games
sleep
drink water
keep yourself clean
wash your hair
clean your teeth twice a day.

<u>Pass the sentence</u>

"'To keep healthy and fit I can…"
Jot down the appropriate things the children say and when all have had their turn read out the list.

<u>Touch your nose</u> if you can think of any more and add these to the list.

Choose one of the things the children said and allow them to elaborate on it. For example if they said 'you have to exercise' – ask children to tell you some of the ways they do this.

<u>Further work</u>

Ask the children to draw themselves doing something that makes and keeps them healthy – use their drawings to make a large picture, mount them individually or send them home with the message that you are learning about how to keep healthy.

6. Keeping my body healthy and safe

Before Circle Time ask all the children to draw a healthy person. Ask them to write around the picture what their person can do to make themselves healthy and keep themselves healthy.

<u>Show and tell</u>

Ask the children to show their pictures and tell one of the things they wrote down.

Jot down a list of the healthy activities the children mention.

Read the list to the children, when all who wish have had a turn. Perhaps these activities can be grouped together under headings such as food, exercise, drink, rest, cleanliness, medical help. (They may include things under mental health or wellbeing such as love, friendship.)

<u>Share ideas</u>

Divide the children into groups, giving each group one of the above healthy activities to explore. Allow the groups to have a few minutes to share ideas and come together in the circle again.

<u>Stand and tell</u>

Ask each group in turn to tell the others what they think is important about their healthy activity. Children can be invited to add suggestions.

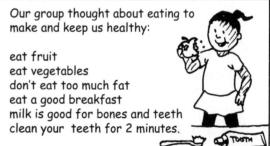

Our group thought about eating to make and keep us healthy:

eat fruit
eat vegetables
don't eat too much fat
eat a good breakfast
milk is good for bones and teeth
clean your teeth for 2 minutes.

<u>Further work</u>

Ask the children to think of any other things that affect our well being. They may offer such things as having friends or pets, being loved, being part of a family, thinking of others and learning new skills. They may mention things you shouldn't do – such as smoking or taking drugs.

7. People I need to keep safe from

Tell the children that you remember their list of people who keep them safe, but that they might need to keep themselves safe from some children or grown-ups.

Ask the children to
<u>touch their shoulders</u> if they have ever been hurt by a child.
<u>touch their ears</u> if they have ever been hurt by an adult.

<u>I keep myself safe from children who</u>...

play football

                                push

  run fast

                    want to fight

don't look where they're going

                    bully people.

<u>Pass the sentence</u>
Tell the children that sometimes people don't mean to hurt – it can happen by accident.
Think about the school playground when there are lots of children playing games.
"In the playground I keep myself safe by...
Jot down what they say and look at your list when all the children have had a turn.

Ask the children to think of people outside school who they might need to keep safe from. Remind them about people who might want to take them away and hurt them and tell the children than they must only go with people who they know are safe.
<u>Pass the sentence</u>
"I go home from school with ...

<u>Further work</u>
Extend this work by talking about your school's policy about bullying. Discuss what they must do if someone they don't know wants to take them home or brings a message that might not be true.
You could talk about good and bad touches and remind them that their body is theirs and they are in charge of who touches them.

7. People I need to keep safe from

Things to say to a bully.

No
Go away
^ That's wrong
No I'm not going to
I'm not afraid of you
I shall tell a grown-up.

Ask children to think of people who might want to harm them and make sure they know what to do if that someone tries to take them away. (e.g. say no, shout loud, run away, find a safe adult, find a safe place.)

<u>Pass the sentence</u>
"If someone wants to hurt me or take me away I must…

Now ask the children to think of other children who might want to harm them or other children – bullies.

Find out what they know about bullies and if they know what to do.

Divide the class into two and use one of these 'pass the sentence' techniques with each half.

<u>Pass the sentence</u>
1. "A bully is someone who…"
2. "If someone tries to bully me I must…"

Ask the children to think of a slogan that will tell everyone what to do if they are bullied.

Give a minute for the children to think and then invite them to :

<u>Stand and tell</u>

Write down the slogans and at the end choose the one most likely to succeed. If no-one is able to think of a slogan, try to work one out with them – "If someone bullies you tell and keep on telling until someone listens."

<u>Further work</u>

Ask the children to fold a piece of paper into two. On the left side ask them to draw a picture of someone who is being bullied and to write what is happening. On the right side ask them to draw someone giving some good advice to the bullied person. Use a speech bubble for the advice. Ask the children to take the work home to show their families or use it to make a wall display.

8. Our messages about Keeping Safe

Remind the children about all the work they have done about keeping themselves safe – at home, in school, from dangerous places and dangerous people.

Ask the children to think of something they could say to other children to help them to keep safe.

<u>Pass the sentence</u>
"I would say…"
Play the <u>change places</u> game if children repeat what has been said.

Keeping safe
messages

Look where you're
going
Don't bump into
people
Hot things burn
Rivers can be deep
Take care near water
Be careful near
strange dogs.

Jot down what the children say.
When all the children have had their turn read out your list of messages.
Focus on a few (three or four) of most appropriate messages and ask the children to choose the one message they think is the best for them.

<u>Stand and count</u>
Read out each of the three or four messages and ask the children who think that is the best for them to stand up and say "I think this is the most important message for me." Ask these children to count themselves.

Make a display of the children's messages and read them with the children frequently.

<u>Further work</u>
Ask the children to think of some time when they were hurt (or when someone else was hurt) and to think whether this was their own fault -because they were not keeping themselves safe. Ask the children to draw what happened next.

8. Our messages about Keeping Safe

Ask children to think of a 'keeping safe message' for the younger children in your school. It can be to do with any aspect of keeping safe.

<u>Stand and tell</u>
> "A good keeping safe message would be …"
> Write the messages on the chalk board.
> Read out these messages with the children.

<u>Share ideas</u>
> Ask the children to leave the circle and go into working groups.
> Ask them to decide which for them is the best keeping safe message.
> Ask them to jot this down together with ideas of how they could make this into a display for younger children in the school. Allow only 4 minutes for this activity.

<u>Stand and tell.</u>
> Come together as a whole class and ask a child from each group to tell everyone their message.
> "Our keeping safe message is…"

<u>Further work.</u>
> Ask the groups to write out their messages and illustrate them.
> Perhaps a small group of children could take their messages to show the younger children.
> They could then display them in an area of the school where everyone will see them.

1. Why do we need rules?

Ask the children to think about how you organise the classroom and what rules you have.
Give them examples such as what do you do:

- with wet paintings
- finished work
- at register time
- when play is over
- when people want to change activities
- about shouting/fighting
- in Circle Time ?

10 children think the important rule for Circle-time is to listen carefully.

Pass the sentence
"A classroom/school rule is…"
Jot down what they say and when they have all had a turn, read out the rules.
You may want to add another one or two.

Ask them to choose which for them is the most important rule from your list.

Stand up/count/sit down
Ask all children to stand.
If they chose the first rule on your list they raise a hand, and count themselves.
As the children count themselves write the number against the rule.
Tell these children to sit down.
Go through your list until all the children are sitting.
Make a display with this data, adding children's pictures or pictures from magazines.

Further work
Ask the children to draw a picture of themselves keeping one of the rules.
Display this work alongside your list of rules.

1. Why do we need rules?

Ask children to think what might happen if we didn't have any rules at all.
Give some examples – such as:

> what might happen on roads if we didn't keep to the left and obey signals
> what could happen in shops if we didn't queue.

<u>Pass the sentence</u>

"If we didn't have rules… "

Share ideas. When all the children have had
their turn ask them to think of the important
rules you have in school or in the classroom.
Ask the children to go into groups to talk about
classroom rules and to jot down what they think
are the three most important rules in the classroom.

> <u>We think the 3 important rules in our</u>
> <u>classroom are:</u>
>
> 1. work quietly
> 2. wait your turn
> 3. listen to others.
>
> Ajit, Bob, Asher, Liam, Shola, Kerm.

Come back together and ask each group to stand up while one child tells their group's three
most important rules.

<u>Further work</u>

Children could vote on the one most important rule or put rules in their order of importance.
Ask children to look out for safety rules they might see when they are out and about.
For example "No cycling" "Danger".

2. Rules outside school

Remind the children about the rules you have in school and tell them one of your own home rules. Ask them to think of one rule they have in school.

<u>Pass the sentence</u>
"One rule we have at school is…"
Stand up, change places
if you know what would happen if you broke the rule you told us.

Home rules

Wipe your shoes on the mat when you come indoors.

Sam

Now ask the children to think of rules we have outside school.

<u>Pass the sentence</u>
"My outside school rule is…"

<u>Stand up, change places</u>
if you know what might happen if you broke that rule.
(You might like to explore this further if the children want to talk about it.)

<u>Further work</u>
Write up the "outside school" rules that you consider important. Read these with the children.
Explore, with the children the rules of various places and situations – e.g. the library, on a bus, in a restaurant, on a picnic, at the seaside, at the dentist, in someone's house, with a dog, with a bicycle.

2. Rules outside school

Ask children to think of the rules in your city, town or village.
Tell them that these are often called laws or by-laws.
Can they think of a rule children have to remember?

A rule is not to take things that don't belong to you.

Krishna

Stand and tell
"We have to remember…"

Can they think of a rule that grown-ups have to remember?

Pass the sentence
"A rule or law that grown-ups have to remember is…"

Policemen help us to keep some rules. They stop people from driving too fast.

Stand and tell
about any people whose job it is to
help us to keep these rules.

Stand up, change places
if you know what might happen to grown ups
who break rules or laws.

Further work
Help the children to find out about local laws.
How do people know about them?
Are there reminders (notices) to keep laws anywhere in your area?
How do people try to make sure they are kept?
What happens to people who don't keep them?

3. Who makes the rules?

Ask the children to think about the rules they have been
talking about in other Circle Times.
Ask them to <u>stand up</u> if they can say who makes the
rules for the school.

Jot down what these children say.
Read your list and ask if they know who is in charge of the whole school.
Does that person make all the rules?
Explain about higher authorities and that even
important people in your school have to obey rules.

<u>Stand and tell</u> if you think having rules is a good idea.
Ask why we need rules at school.

<u>Pass the sentence</u>
"I think we need rules because...."

Ask the children to think of what might happen if we did not have rules at school.
<u>Pass the sentence</u>
"I think if we didn't have rules…"

<u>Further work</u>
Ask the children to think of some good rules for playing outside school.
Ask them to decide (vote) on the best rule to put into practice.
Display this new rule surrounded by pictures drawn by the children showing them obeying it.

School rules
Our teachers make some rules.
Our headteacher makes some rules.
Governors make some rules.
The local office people make some rules.
The government make some rules.

Rules are a good idea. They help us to know what to do.

3. Who makes the rules?

> People make local laws in the town hall. They are called councillors.

Ask children to think of the by-laws and laws that we have.
<u>Stand and tell</u> if you think you know who made them.
Jot down what the children say. Read your list.

Ask the children to think of how people agree about which laws to make, and to
<u>Stand up and tell</u> if they can say how people decide.

Help the children to understand about voting and democratic decisions and that even when people don't agree they have to abide by the decision of the majority.
Compare this to how school decisions are made by teachers and governors.
Compare this to how you and the children make decisions about things in class.

Ask the children to think of what could happen if we did not have laws.
<u>Pass the sentence</u>
"If we didn't have laws…"

Finally ask the children to think about what should happen to people who break laws.
Ask them to focus on one rule or law. What would they do to someone who broke it.
<u>Pass the sentence</u>
"If someone broke…. rule/law I think they should…"

<u>Further work</u>
Bring in some materials to help them to find out about local councillors.
Can they find leaflets or photographs in the paper?
Ask them to write about the job of councillor. Make a display of this work.
If possible, arrange a visit to the local magistrate's or county court.
Ask a local magistrate to come to school to talk to the children about their work.
Talk about the jury system.

Go to prison

4. Other people's property and feelings

Remind the children that they have to take care of things that belong to other people as well as things that belong to them. Ask if they can remember having something that belonged to someone else and how they took care of it.
<u>Stand up/change places</u>

<u>Tell the children this story:</u>
> *Ranjit had borrowed a book from the library and he read it in his room. He went downstairs for a drink of coke and his Mum told him to drink it downstairs and not to spill it. He went back for his book and was reading it when his baby sister toddled over to him. She pulled his arm and the drink spilt – all over the library book.*

How do you think Ranjit, his Mum, the Librarian and the baby sister felt?

<u>Pass the sentence</u>
"I think… felt…"

Oh
NO!

<u>Stand and tell</u>
if you can think what Ranjit should do.
Jot down what the children say.
Read your list and ask the children to tell you what they think is the best thing Ranjit could do.

We think Ranjit should:

dry the book
tell the Librarian and say 'sorry'
say he would buy another book
make sure he was more careful next time

<u>Further work</u>
Talk about other similar disasters and discuss what could be done to repair the situation.
Tell the children that saying 'sorry' is a good idea.
Ask how can they make sure it doesn't happen again.

4. Other people's property and feelings

Ask children how they feel when they break/spoil things or when they see broken things.

<u>Pass the sentence</u> – choose one of the following, or use both for half the children.
    "When I see broken things I feel…"
    "When I break/spoil things I feel…"

Explore some of the words the children used.
Did some of the words mean the same?
Did some mean the opposite?
Did some children use the same words to complete both the sentences?

Ask the children to think of a time when they had to take great care of something very special.
<u>Stand and tell</u> what happened.

Remind the children that even when things are not especially
precious they should take care not to break or spoil them.
Ask the children to think of something they always have to take great care of.
<u>Pass the sentence</u>
    "I always take care of…"

<u>Further work</u>
    Remind the children that other people's feelings are
    important too and that they have to take care of them.
    Ask if they can remember when someone hurt their
    feelings or when they hurt someone's feelings.
    How did they feel? What did they do to make things better?
    Make a display of children's drawings and writing on this theme for parents & other children.

When I hurt Sara's feelings she cried. I said I was sorry.

5. Being truthful

Ask the children if they have ever found it difficult to tell the truth because they were afraid of getting into trouble. Tell them that we all make mistakes and that it is only fair to own up to them and to say we are sorry. (If you can, tell of some experience of yours when it was difficult for you to own up.)

Ask the children to think of how their face looked when they were not telling the truth.
<u>Pass the face</u> round the circle.
Tell them that a good way to tell the truth is to start by saying "Yes, I'm sorry…

Ask the children to tell of some time when they were sorry about something.

I showed I was sorry:

I said I'd not do it again
I tried to mend it
I said I didn't mean it
I gave my Mum a kiss
I cleared up the mess
I'll try to be more careful
I'll think before I do things
I'll watch what I'm doing.

<u>Pass the sentence</u>
"I was sorry when…"

Tell the children that it is hard sometimes to say sorry, even when they feel sorry inside.
Ask them to think of a way that people can show they are sorry.
<u>Stand and tell</u>

<u>Further work</u>
Ask the children to think of some time when it was hard to tell the truth. Talk about 'owning up', and that people won't believe anything you say if they know you tell lies. Ask them to draw a picture of themselves telling the truth.

5. Being truthful

Ask children to think of a time when they found it hard to 'own up' to doing something.
<u>Pass the face</u> to show how you felt.

It was hard to own up...
I felt:

sad
embarrassed
unhappy
it was an accident
scared I'd be in trouble
angry with myself
fed up.

Can they think of a word to describe how they felt?
<u>Stand and tell</u>
Collect the words they give you and read them back.

Repeat the above, this time asking the children to tell
how they felt when they had owned up and told the truth.

After I told the truth
I felt:

better
relieved
glad
wonderful
warm inside
I could smile again.

Talk about the difference between acting/pretending and real life.
Ask the children to tell about what they like to pretend to do or be.

<u>Pass the sentence</u>
"I like to pretend… but it's not the truth."

<u>Further work</u>
Make two charts to display the words the children gave you about how they felt:
       when they found it hard to own up
       after they had owned up.
Ask the children to work in pairs to write about why it is important to tell the truth.
Display some of this work around your two charts.
Read or tell the story about the boy who cried 'wolf'.

6. Losing and finding

I felt very sad when I lost my teddy. I cried.

Ask the children to
<u>Stand up</u> if they have ever lost anything.

Ask them to tell you what they lost and how they felt.
<u>Stand and tell</u>

Now ask them how they felt when they found it (or something they had lost) again.
<u>Pass the sentence</u>
"When I found it I felt…

Now ask them if they have ever found anything that belonged to someone else.
<u>Stand and tell</u>
Remind them how the person might have felt if they lost something they treasured.

Ask them to choose and finish one of these sentences.
<u>Pass the sentence</u>
"If you find something you should…"
"If you find something you shouldn't…"

When I found my toy car I felt so glad and happy again.

<u>Further work</u>
Ask the children to draw a picture of themselves:
either with something they have either lost or something they found.
Ask the children to tell you of their feelings when they lost or found this object (or person).
Display their pictures in the two groups with the words they told you in large speech bubbles.
Read stories to the children on this theme – such as
"Dogger", by S. Hughes, published by Red Fox.

94

6. Losing and finding

Ask the children to think about how they feel when they lose something.

<u>Pass the sentence</u>

"When I lose something I feel…"

Now ask children to think of some of the things they might find when they are out and about. Remind them that these things could be valuable, interesting, dirty, dangerous.

<u>Pass the sentence</u>

"If you find something valuable you should…"

"If you find something interesting you should…"

"If you find something dirty you should…"

"If you find something dangerous you should…"

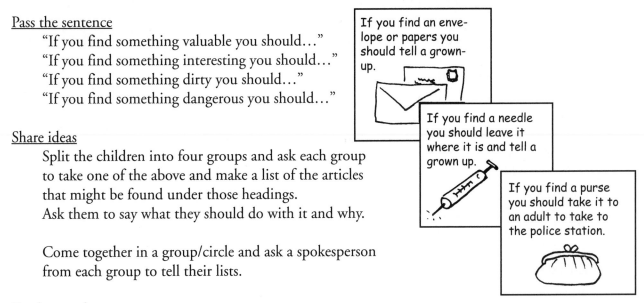

If you find an envelope or papers you should tell a grown-up.

If you find a needle you should leave it where it is and tell a grown up.

If you find a purse you should take it to an adult to take to the police station.

<u>Share ideas</u>

Split the children into four groups and ask each group to take one of the above and make a list of the articles that might be found under those headings.

Ask them to say what they should do with it and why.

Come together in a group/circle and ask a spokesperson from each group to tell their lists.

<u>Further work</u>

Talk to the children of the dangers of touching dangerous objects such as needles, syringes or spent cartridges. Make sure they know what to do.

7. Litter

Ask the children to think about what to do with things they no longer want to keep –such as ice cream papers or sweet wrappers.

Ask them to
> stand up if they should throw them down in the street
> stand up if they should put them in a litter bin
> stand up if they should take them home with them

How do they feel when they see litter?

<u>Pass the sentence</u>
"When I see litter I feel…"
"When I see litter I think…"

What do they think happens to things that are thrown away?

<u>Stand and tell</u>

<u>Further work</u>
Talk to the children about things that can be recycled and what happens to things that cannot be recycled e.g. dumped in a great hole and covered over.

Ask the children to tell you if they can think of anything old that their family uses again for a different purpose.

We think litter is:

Yuk!

horrid
awful
disgusting
messy
smelly
horrible
spoils things
makes things look bad.

Don't drop it - ever.

7. Litter

Talk to children about litter and the way some people drop it just anywhere.

What would they say to people who drop litter?

<u>Pass the sentence</u>

"I would say….."

Now talk to them about the difficulties of disposing of unwanted goods.

Ask them to think of what people can do with things they no longer want.

<u>Pass the sentence</u>

"If you don't want it any more, you could…"

Remind the children that we sometimes use junk materials to make things.

<u>Share ideas</u>

Ask them to work in pairs or threes and make a list of all the different bits of junk they have used to make things.

After 3 minutes ask one child from each group to stand up and read out their list.

<u>Further work</u>

This could include finding out about their local rubbish disposal.

Are there tips or dumps for large item such as beds?

Does their local authority have a garden waste recycling programme?

Who wants old clothes?

What happens to school rubbish?

Get rid of things you
don't want this way:

sell them
take to charity shops
recycle it yourself
put them in the dustbin
take them to the dump
put them in recycle sacks
take to garden waste dump
take to recycling bins.

8. Protect our environment

Ask the children if they know what the word environment means.
<u>Stand up and tell</u> if you know.

Collect up what they say. If no-one knows, explain that it means the surroundings – the area around where we live, the natural world and the countryside.

Ask the children to think of all the beautiful things in our environment .
<u>Pass the sentence</u>

"Our environment is beautiful because…"
Jot down what the children say.

When children repeat what has been said they
<u>Change places</u> with the last person to say it.

Ask the children to <u>Stand up and tell</u> if they can think of someone who is responsible for keeping the environment looking good.

Ask the children what they themselves can do.
<u>Pass the sentence</u>

"We can…."

<u>Further work</u>

Ask the children to look around the school and grounds for things that have been put there to make it more beautiful. Can they make a list of them?

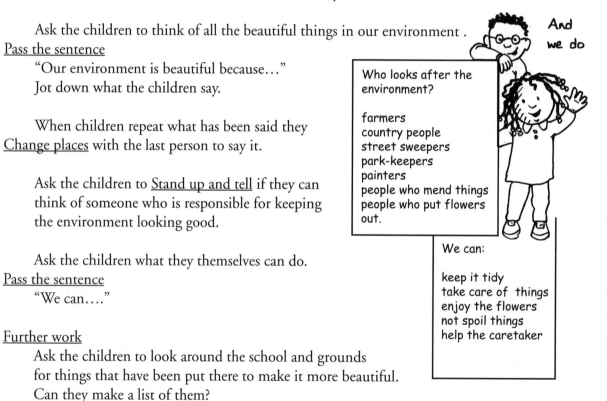

And we do

Who looks after the environment?

farmers
country people
street sweepers
park-keepers
painters
people who mend things
people who put flowers out.

We can:

keep it tidy
take care of things
enjoy the flowers
not spoil things
help the caretaker

8. Protect our environment

Ask children to think of one thing they can do to keep
their school environment looking good.

<u>Pass the sentence</u>
"To keep our school environment looking good I could…"
Jot down what the children say, noting the number of repeats.

Ask the children if they know who makes, mends or puts
beautiful and interesting things in our environment,
(e.g. street furniture such as seats, plants, notices).

<u>Stand and tell.</u>
Collect the children's responses and use these to
make a list of 'environment improvers'.

> <u>Environment improvers</u>
>
> Shopkeepers put flowers
> outside.
> The council people put seats
> and litter boxes.
> Dustbin men empty our rubbish
> away.
> Street sweepers clean the
> roads and pavements
> People mend the lights.
> People paint the lamp-posts.
> People plant trees and flowers.

Remind the children that some people spoil the environment by leaving litter, breaking things
or spraying with spray paints.
Ask them to stand up if they think they will spoil things when they are bigger.

Ask what they think of people who do that.

<u>Pass the sentence</u>
"I think …"

<u>Further work</u>
Ask the children to look around your locality for things that have been put there to make it
more attractive. You could take the children on a 'looking walk' around the school grounds or
locality. Make a list of all the things that make your environment more beautiful.

Resources

Purr...fect Skills

To assist with the development of Social Skills our publication, 'Purr...fect Skills - Social Skills Key Stage 1', uses the story of two kittens: one who has been in Cat School for one year and is helping prepare her sister, who is just about to start school, for the skills she will have to learn. The pack provides stories, worksheets and teacher instructions to cover skills such as:

- Taking turns,
- Awareness of feelings,
- Making and keeping friends.

The pack also includes two hand puppets.

Song Books

These song books contain songs that will provide interesting fun ways to end the Circle Time sessions.

Apusskidu - songs for children 56 songs. A. & C. Black, London 1975.

Bingo Lingo - supporting language development with songs and rhymes by Helen MacGregor. A. & C. Black, 1999.

Bobby Shafto Clap Your Hands by Sue Nicholls. A & C Black, 1992.

Count Me In - 44 Songs & Rhymes about numbers. A. & C. Black, London, 1984.

Game Songs by Harriet Powell. A. & C. Black, London, 1983.

Harlequin - 44 songs round the year. A. & C. Black, London, 1981.

High Low Dolly Pepper by Veronica Clark. A. & C. Black, London, 1991.

Jim along Josie by Nancy & John Langstaff. OUP, London, 1970.

Okki Tokki Unga - Action songs for children. A & C Black, 1978.

Primrose Early Years Pack by Barbara Lipscomb, Primrose Publications Ltd., Lancaster. 1995.

Tinderbox - 66 songs for children, A. & C. Black, 1987.

Circle Time

The following publications are available from Lucky Duck Publishing Ltd. They provide a range of resources:

an introduction to the process for new comers

developing more activities for those with some experience

a progressive curriculum for experienced Circle Time enthusiasts.

- Circle Time
- Developing Circle Time
- Coming Round to Circle Time (training video)
- Six Years of Circle Time
- Magic Circles
- Circle Time Resources
- Circle Time for the Very Young.

The author, Margaret Collins, has written or contributed to the following publications:

Keeping Safe - safety education for young children. M. Collins. Forbes Publications Ltd. 1995.

Keep yourself safe - an activity based resource for primary schools. M. Collins. Lucky Duck Publishing Ltd. 1997.

Let's get it right for Nursery Children. M. Collins. Forbes Publications 1998.

Ourselves Resource Pack. (Watch), N. Wetton & M. Collins. "BBC Educational Publishing 1998.

Birth Care and Growth Resource Pack (Watch), N. Wetton & M. Collins, "BBC Educational Publishing. 1999.

Health for Life, Ages 4-7. N. Wetton, T. Williams. Nelson. 2000.

Don't forget to visit our website for all our latest publications, news and reviews.

www.luckyduck.co.uk

New publications every year on our specialist topics:

▸ **Emotional Literacy**

▸ **Self-esteem**

▸ **Bullying**

▸ **Positive Behaviour Management**

▸ **Circle Time**

▸ **Anger Management**

▸ **Asperger's Syndrome**

▸ **Eating Disorders**

3 Thorndale Mews, Clifton, Bristol, BS8 2HX | Tel: +44 (0) 117 973 2881 Fax: +44 (0) 117 973 1707